Deme

Pastoral Theology and Pastoral Care

James Saunders

Assistant Curate
The Sole Bay Team Ministry, East Suffolk

GROVE BOOKS LIMITED
RIDLEY HALL RD CAMBRIDGE CB3 9HU

Contents

Acknowledgments

Many people have helped with this booklet. I am sorry there is not enough space to mention everyone. However, I must record my special indebtedness to Mike Burke, David Clough, Stephen Burns, Graham Owen, Philip Plyming, and Professor Stephen Sykes.

The Cover Illustration is by Peter Ashton

First Impression March 2002
ISSN 0144-171X
ISBN 1 85174 492 4

1

Questions of Pastoral Theology

Asking the Questions

I remember my first encounter with dementia clearly. I was exploring the possibility of ordination and so spending time with my local minister, seeing what he got up to. One of the first things Greg and I did together was spend an hour giving communion to residents of a nursing home in our parish. In the last rooms we came to were two very elderly women, sunk in the deep isolation which accompanies late-stage Alzheimer's Disease. They were staring blankly and fixedly ahead and gave no signs of noticing we were there. They had no reaction when we said the Lord's Prayer, nor when we slipped a fragment of bread and a few drops of wine between their lips. They swallowed, by simple reflex. There was no observable sign they had gained anything from receiving the sacrament, indeed no sign they even noticed we had been there. A thin line of wine dribbled down one woman's cardigan front, so we mopped it off and left. Standing back on the street, I spoke briefly to Greg about what, for him, was a monthly encounter. 'If you can ever tell me what we're meant to be doing there,' said Greg, 'then I'd really like to know.'

I have come back to that question numerous times, first as a care assistant and now as a minister. What *does* the church imagine it is doing through its sacramental and pastoral ministries for people who suffer severe forms of dementia? Should it bother doing anything at all?

For Greg, and many like him who are assiduous and caring pastors there is an almost instinctive feeling that we *ought* to carry on offering communion to anyone used to receiving it, for as long as they remain capable of swallowing. But is this any more than vague sentiment or something designed primarily for public consumption—a sign to relatives and wider society that the church does not abandon its own? Is it bad theology to give the sacraments to people who have no understanding of, or response to what is going on?

Pastoral Care or Pastoral Neglect?

As I have asked myself questions like these over the years, I have gradually come to wish that more Christians could ask them, more often. A Church of England report concluded in 1990 that 'Christian theology and the practice of the church...both seem tacitly to exclude the person with dementia.'[1] Other bodies have pointed out the almost total absence of dementia sufferers from churches and the effective abandonment of life-long church members as soon as nursing-home doors shut behind them. Memories of my own time working as a care assistant include the frustration of telling local ministers that someone of their denomination had arrived in our specialist unit for people with dementia but so rarely seeing any church representative visit. No one, of course, said they would not visit someone with dementia—but no one actually came either. At times it could feel as if Christians who proclaimed belief in life after the body's death lacked concern for the life still persisting in the demented body.

The Dilemmas of Pastoral Care

Nowadays, I am more sympathetic to the dilemmas of pastoral care. Those responsible for visiting are overstretched; people with dementia tend to be hidden away in their homes and hospitals; visiting someone with dementia can be very challenging. I have heard relatives of people suffering from dementia say that the person they knew 'died years ago,' and if those most intimate with someone suffering from dementia can suggest the person they loved is 'dead,' it is hardly surprising that over-stretched pastors, thankful to avoid a difficult and unrewarding visit, act on the premise.

All this is true, and yet, I would suggest, not the whole truth. Perhaps if we look deep into ourselves and our models of ministry, then we might find more profound reasons for the church's failure to meet the needs of people with dementia. Issues of time-management and pastoral priority can seem petty, but behind them lie profound questions of the ultimate value of human beings, their relationship with God, and their relationships with each other—fundamentals of all pastoral theology. We stand little chance of moving beyond benign neglect of people with dementia unless we begin to recognize the questions and find some answers. Without a firm theological commitment to care for the person with dementia it will always be the lack of time for visiting, the trepidation which grips us on walking into a room full of confused people, and the thought that 'the visit will be forgotten within seconds anyway' which will determine our pastoral responses. It is one of the aims of this booklet to encourage us all to develop that necessary theological commitment.

2
Dementia

Just about everyone who picks up this booklet will have come into contact with dementia. Perhaps the rather smart elderly woman two doors down started looking dishevelled and went to live with her son. Perhaps we were visiting a friend in hospital and became distracted by a man who was always looking for the door but never found it. Or perhaps our own mother or father is increasingly forgetful and unable to cope with everyday tasks.

Dementia is common in societies with a high life-expectancy, and a significant cause of disability among the elderly. In the United Kingdom, as many as 800,000 people have identifiable symptoms. Although it is usually found in people aged sixty-five and over (and in one in four people aged over eighty), presenile dementias in people as young as their twenties are not unknown.

Medically, the term 'dementia' is used to describe a number of conditions which exhibit very similar symptoms rather than one disease with a single cause. Diagnosis is usually made from observations which show that a person is suffering 'global impairment of cognition'—in other words, difficulties in performing a whole range of brain-related activities, such as remembering things or putting events into their correct sequence. The underlying cause of these difficulties is progressive, irreversible and eventually catastrophic wasting of the brain tissues.

In around 60% of cases, this wasting is attributable to Alzheimer's Disease. Multi-Infarct Dementia (caused by numerous tiny bleeds in the brain) accounts for around 20% of cases. Other, less common, dementing illnesses include Lewy Body dementia, Pick's Disease and Creuzfeldt-Jakob Disease (CJD). Dementia can also be a feature of Parkinson's Disease, HIV–AIDS, Down's Syndrome, and Multiple Sclerosis, or can be brought on by prolonged alcoholism (Korsakoff's Syndrome).

The Experience of Dementia

Though the medical diagnosis of dementia is based on symptoms common to many people, the experience of the illness is highly individual. The speed of neurological wasting, the areas of the brain it affects, the ability of a sufferer to compensate for consequent losses, the extent to which he or she is supported, and the environment in which he or she lives all have their effect. Those of us who are healthy can only crudely understand what it is like to suffer from dementia. It is a mistake—if, unfortunately, a common one—to assume that all people with dementia suffer in the same way and have the same needs. Nonetheless, if we want our pastoral care to be of a high quality, it is helpful to have some idea of experiences and feelings they are likely to encounter.

The first thing that friends or relatives of a person with dementia usually notice is an unaccustomed forgetfulness on the part of the person they know. At first it can be difficult to tell whether this is something sinister or just a part of normal ageing. Sooner or later, though, it will become apparent that the problem is worsening and that the person is finding it difficult to process the thousands of pieces of new information which they meet every day. The condition may progress until short-term memory is almost non-existent, and life is lived in the past or an 'eternal "now."'¹ As Diana Friel McGowin expresses it in a book describing the course of her own dementia, life 'had become an improvisational theatre, and I was left to ad lib my way through it.'² People met two minutes before are not remembered; the ten steps from the bedroom to the lounge cannot be retraced without help. Gradually, the memories which are accessible to the sufferer become more and more distant and childhood is relived—carers are mistaken for parents, sons and daughters are not recognized. Such severely compromised memory and processing abilities produce disorientation in time and place, frequent misperception, and problems sequencing actions correctly. Sufferers may wander in vain for recognizable landmarks or sit on a bookcase, mistaking it for a chair. They may be unable to dress themselves without prompting.

Coping with a world when so many normal interpretative cues are unavailable is exhausting and stressful. Maintaining any kind of function takes enormous effort, particularly where neurological decline brings about deterioration in a person's fine motor skills, balance, speech, bladder and bowel control. The combination of declining brain function, an ever-more bewildering environment, and huge personal stress force the sufferer to find ways of coping with the experience. Perhaps we can understand why dementia sufferers are often said to undergo personality changes, becoming emotionally volatile or retreating further and further into themselves. The social self—the sophisticated public face we all present to the world—is high-maintenance and demands energies and capabilities which someone struggling to keep going does not have available. Depression, aggression, anxiety, paranoia, disinhibited behaviour, lack of interest in self-care and confabulation (the invention of narratives to make sense of reality as it is (mis)perceived) are common reactions to the stresses experienced.

As we have said, the experience of dementia is ultimately an individual one. Some sufferers are merely 'pleasantly muddled.' For others, however, the experience can be embarrassing, frightening and exhausting, and Glen Weaver's description of dementia as a 'return to chaos' may be helpful, reminding us of the profound confusion and sense of disintegration which dementia can bring. It is understandable that observers often use a vocabulary of irrationality and unpredictability to describe the symptoms of dementia. Yet from within, dementia can be much more distressing than talk of detachment from the real world might suggest. The experience is of a desperate search for order with which to hold off threatening chaos; of endless improvisation as one longs for stability and time; and of life in the 'eternal "now"' while seeking to fix a past and a future. Although drifting apart from the world, the dementia sufferer is trying desperately to maintain contact.

Dementia and Society

Sometimes, genuine obstacles prevent a person with dementia venturing out of doors, but in the main there is no reason why we should not expect to see even people with quite advanced dementia out shopping, travelling on a bus, or eating in the pub with family and friends. Given the opportunities and some sympathetic help, people with dementia can still flourish as human beings, despite their incapacities. Yet it does not usually happen like that.

One of the most important realizations among dementia specialists in recent years has been how difficult we all make it for the person with dementia to play a part in the world. In seminal work, the late Tom Kitwood explored the far-reaching consequences of the conceptual models by which society interprets dementia.[3] Firstly, he suggested our faith in an all-knowing medical science leads us to conclude that a *diagnosis* of dementia is an adequate description of the *prognosis* for the sufferer. And secondly, he argued, this misplaced faith causes us to neglect the social history of the disease (the extent to which, in reality, prognosis is determined by individual and environmental factors). We imagine, in other words, that the disease somehow *defines* the identity of the individual, and allow it to swallow up the person. The impact of this, Kitwood contends, has been disastrous. It has led people in our care systems to be treated as the biological 'objects' of medical science—objects which need physical care and 'management,' but little else.

If you have visited a nursing home or hospital where this is the underlying attitude, you are likely to have sensed what it means in practice. The demands of the institution for standardization, routine, and financial efficiency are given priority over the human needs of the patient. You may have seen dementia sufferers sat all day in front of the television, moved only to be brought to table or the toilet. You may have noticed human expressions of frustration or desire (such as wandering away from the table at mealtime) being crushed with an increased drug dosage.

Thanks to the work of people like Tom Kitwood, much has been done to improve the care of people with dementia over the last couple of decades, and scenes like these are less common than they once were. Nevertheless, the 'new culture' in dementia care is far from universal. There are still nursing homes and hospitals in which the system demeans, neglects, and occasionally abuses the humanity of people with dementia. In the light of the new understandings of dementia, an urgent task for the church is to ensure that we do not accidentally do the same thing in our own spheres of responsibility.

3
Dementia and Theological Tradition

In our first chapter, we came across some hard questions. Should pastoral care of the dementia sufferer be a priority? Can people with dementia even be considered 'people' at all? The implicit theology of many Christians (in other words, the theological beliefs implied by their (in)action) argues that they do *not* see ministry to people with dementia as important.

If all this is correct, then I think we must work to expose the roots of such implicit theology. Only then can it be effectively challenged. A set of theological understandings unable to conceive of a person with dementia as a 'person' at all is a major handicap to pastoral good practice. It is hard to feel that something is a pastoral priority when the working assumptions of our faith tell us otherwise.

The Church Fathers and the Thomists
For many centuries, one of the most influential legacies to which Christian theology was heir was that of the ascetics. Ascetic traditions tended to be suspicious of 'the flesh' and anything associated with the physical body. They had a marked tendency to look to the realms of the mind and spirit in their search for an uncorrupted core of human existence.

Ascetic suspicions were retained through the great flowering of medieval theology, and beyond. When Thomas Aquinas read the creation narratives in Genesis 1 and 2 and reflected what they implied for an understanding of humanity, he concluded that humanity's capacity for intellectual reasoning was the best evidence we have of our relatedness to God. 'Although in all creatures there is some kind of likeness to God,' he argued in *Summa Theologica* (93.6), 'in the rational creature alone do we find the likeness of *image*…this image of God is not found even in the rational creature except in the mind.'

Aquinas and his followers argued that rationality was evidence of humanity's 'family likeness' to God. Just as my blue eyes and brown hair suggest that I am my mother's son and related to her by blood, so my ability to manipulate logic and reason suggest I am God's child and related to him. Thomists also argued that reason was the channel by which true relationship with God was made possible for humanity. To quote E L Mascall (a twentieth-century Anglican admirer of Aquinas), even God's grace 'is a gift which is only possible to a rational being.'[4]

Classical Reformed Theology
In most respects, classical Protestant theology reacted strongly against scholastic theology such as that of Thomas Aquinas. Protestantism was generally

anxious to emphasize the infinite gulf between God and humanity, and so roundly rejected any belief that human beings could be somehow analogous to God in their possession of cognitive faculties. Protestant theologians were often more ambivalent about Aquinas' assertion that reason was necessary for the establishment of a relationship between God and humanity.

Much Reformed theology was built on a commitment to the importance of conversion, typically described as an event in which a sinner finds relationship with God and so becomes authentically human. The most important element in Reformed descriptions of this event was, undeniably, the unmerited grace of God coming upon the sinner. We are not, they emphasized, saved by any ability or capacity we possess in ourselves, reason included. And yet there often appears to have been a deep-seated unease at the radically unpredictable consequences of this description. As a result, emphasis on the primacy of God's grace was often balanced by a subtle reinsertion of reason into the conversion process. Human beings, it was held, must be aware of their sinfulness and their need for Christ, and must respond to the objective work of the cross. Humanity, in short, must *answer* God's grace in order to enjoy a relationship of perfect trust and obedience with him, and answering requires the understanding given by reason. Twentieth-century theologian Emil Brunner, for example, insisted that salvation comes by faith alone. But faith, he explained, 'is *reason* subject to the rule of God...'[5]

Reason, Conversion, and Humanity

Summarized so baldly, we may all be able to see the inadequacies of Brunner's definition. Seeing it in the context of his other theological commitments, however, might allow us to be a little more sympathetic.

Reformed theology's understanding of human nature was often driven by the missionary imperative. It understood that human beings living apart from God could not realize their full humanity, and that sin had fractured the life-giving relationship with God which people needed so badly. Reformed theology therefore wanted to convince people of their need of God in order to save them, because it believed that all human beings were personally guilty of sin and personally responsible for their actions. And so it was tacitly assumed every human being was rational.

But there are great dangers in this line of argument. Let us imagine a person with dementia and pose a hypothetical question. Arthur does not always act rationally, and if he hits me, he cannot be held responsible for his action, legally or morally. But if Arthur is not responsible because he is no longer in his rational mind, then how can we speak of him coming to 'know' God in faith? And if we lack the vocabulary to speak of this, then how can we still speak of him as human?

The average believer in the pew, of a more practical mind than the average

9

theologian, may not have considered linking questions of moral responsibility and essential humanity. (Though ask whether it is worth the effort of evangelizing someone with dementia to start the debate!) But theologians who have made the link have ended up in murky waters. Emil Brunner's answer to the theological problem was brutally logical. He denied that Arthur and people like him were people at all:

> This formal essential structure [of personal responsibility] cannot be lost. It is identical with human existence as such, and indeed with the quality of being which all human beings possess equally; it only ceases where true human living ceases—on the borderline of imbecility or madness.[6]

Dementia, we could conclude, means death—not just physical death, but the death of human nature itself.

I do not want to suggest that Emil Brunner (or for that matter Thomas Aquinas) was a poor theologian, still less an evil man. As Christians, all of us find it difficult to move beyond the vocabulary of reason, for thinking, reading, reflecting, and communicating—words and ideas—lie at the heart of so much Christian life. It is only when we allow what is *normal* in day-to-day practice to define what is *necessary* that we enter dangerous territory. Abstract theology is inadequate where it fails to take account of pastoral reality, just as our pastoral practice is the poorer when it avoids deep thought about fundamental issues of the human condition.

From Reason to Relationship

This booklet is certainly not the first piece of writing to be critical of the way in which rationality has been treated as a prerequisite of humanity. In the earlier decades of the twentieth century, theologians such as Karl Barth and Martin Büber were expressing dissatisfaction with heavy rationalism, and developing theologies in which relationship rather than reason was understood as the cornerstone of being human.[7] Boiled down to barest essentials, the key argument of both men was that true humanity is dependent on relationship with God and the rest of creation. Authentic humanity is established when two beings meet— a human 'Thou' and a divine 'I.' This fundamental insight launched an entire theological movement (sometimes referred to as 'dialogical personalism') and continues to be enormously influential. Nurture programmes such as *Alpha* or *Emmaus* which emphasize the crucial role of relationship in conversion are just one end-product of the re-thinking which the movement brought about.

The greatest advance of this new understanding from the viewpoint of the dementia sufferer is to direct attention to the particular *qualities* associated with 'I—Thou' relationship. Intimacy, spontaneity and self-giving could now be seen to lie at the core of human existence rather than the rational mind. This fact by itself has led mental health professionals (including Tom Kitwood) to draw on the work of Martin Büber in books arguing for greater recognition of the humanity of people suffering from mental illness.

However, while Barth and Büber undoubtedly mark a great advance for the person with dementia, not everything in their understanding of what it means to be human is entirely helpful.

To speak about 'I' and 'Thou' suggests that we think of 'relationship' as a state which exists between two individuals. But followers of Barth and Büber have argued that in order to be an 'individual' it is not enough for us simply to exist in our own unique way, time and space. To be individual we must also be aware of these things. 'I am' because I *recognize* my own unique existence, because I can *remember* my own past and because I *respond* to the world around me in ways consistent with my own identity.

'So far, so abstract,' we might reckon. But abstractions can give a nasty bite when turned on real people, and the consequences of all this for someone with dementia become clear as Ray Anderson builds on a Barthian scheme in his book *On Being Human*. Anderson tries to explain how humans can be distinguished from animals when animals too are creatures of God. Eventually, he comes to the conclusion that to be human is to have a *capacity for response* in relationship. Mental illness—the loss of a rational nature—he says, threatens this capacity, and so too a human being's unique nature:

> Insanity can be…understood theologically as…a slip into sheer unhistorical creatureliness. It is understandable that this can often happen to persons who have particularly brilliant minds, for the soul, as the differentiation produced by awareness of God, is the essence of rationality; and it only exists as a differentiated response to an awareness of the divine Word.[8]

Anderson's vocabulary is complex, and we need to note carefully the practical implications of what he is saying. Human beings, he is claiming, are only fully human when they are *aware* of themselves as individuals living in response to God. Thus people who are cognitively unaware of what is going on around them and on whom nothing can make any rational impression cannot be described as living an authentically human existence. Somewhere, we feel, reason has returned as a vital ingredient in relationships and understandings of what being human involves.

Real Relationships

We have seen in this chapter that the humanity of people with dementia has often been denied by a theological obsession with rationality which has heavily influenced descriptions of coming to faith and engaging in relationships. The twentieth-century theologians may not necessarily have had a deliberate concern to re-establish reason as a core attribute of being human. But all writers draw on the insights of earlier thinkers and in the discipline of theology the inheritance is stuffed full of the language of thinking, reasoning, and analysing. The vocabulary is difficult to escape even when we try and speak of a concept like 'relationship,' in which the emotions should surely figure much more prominently.

Yet deliberate or not, the consequences are serious. In applying such vocabulary to people suffering from dementia we are forced to presume that true humanity is absent from their aimless and uncomprehending waiting. We must imagine that authentic humanity is not found in Jack as he wanders continuously, lost in impenetrable inner motivations, detached and unreceptive to the world; and that it is not to be detected in Maggie, whose greatest emotional solace comes from chattering to her own image in the mirror. Those suffering from severe forms of dementia are reduced to objects, undifferentiated biological machines which exist alongside us, rather than living *with* us.

And yet my experience tells me that in caring for Jack, Maggie, and those like them I *have* enjoyed relationships with them. They may not have been able to identify me, remember me, or even respond coherently, but I will insist that these relationships felt intimate and genuine. The experience of working with people suffering from dementia seems to tell me a different story from the theological analysis. It is a story in which real love and instinctive empathy feature prominently, in which I can feel love for people who do not respond to it, and in which the possibility that breathing, embodied people are 'dead' seems frankly incredible. The task now is to catch up with this experience.

4
Jesus' Healing Ministry

It is time for the author to own up! I have a strongly held personal opinion that developments in Western theology such as those outlined in the previous chapter have effectively forged the church's very own culture of denial and exclusion for men and women with dementia. I think it is now time that we tried to point the way towards a more inclusive theology. Chapter five will try to indicate what this might mean in the language of 'systematic' theology, but I think it is important that first of all we go to the gospels, as the founding documents of our faith. As space is limited my focus in this chapter will be Jesus' healing ministry.[9] Despite the narrowness of this approach, I hope that there is enough in the healing narratives to throw into sharp relief some of the inadequacies of the theological developments explored in the previous chapter, and to offer a biblical grounding for approaches I suggest in the next.

The Healing Touch
We have begun to realize how isolated from mainstream society and the church people with dementia can be. In contrast, Jesus' ministry in the synoptic gospels is undertaken in the very midst of the dirt, sin and sweating crowds. The salvation which Jesus offers is not something merely existential or metaphysical, but God's commitment to the real world. One of the most obvious and most fundamental aspects of Jesus' healings is the plain fact that he is *there*, in the flesh, for the world. In Christ, God comes visibly and tangibly alongside his people to bring healing. The gospel writers show this by their emphasis on Jesus *touching* those he heals. He takes Simon Peter's mother-in-law by the hand (Mark 1.31), rubs saliva into a blind man's eyes (8.22, 25), and even heals as he is touched by people he has not seen (5.28–29; 6.56).

Healing the Whole Person
We have also begun to realize that people with dementia suffer because people assume that the illness they suffer swallows them up, reducing their personality to their symptoms. Care, in this climate, has sometimes involved nothing more than the management of these symptoms. In contrast, healings brought about by the touch of Jesus' body signify something deeper than the cure of a physical malady. When, in Luke 5.13, Jesus lays his hand on a leper he is to cure, the touch is a powerful sign that the leper's enforced separation from his community is at an end, and that reintegration into normal society is now possible. Something similar happens a little later when Jesus sits to eat with Levi and other pariahs of the day (Luke 5.29–32). Though suffering no physical illness,

they too are 'healed' (note the vocabulary of v 31) for their inclusion in the new community based around Jesus is a restoration of their relationship with God.

This insight may help us make sense of links often made in the gospels between sinfulness, demon-possession, and sickness. Healing in Jesus' ministry was healing of the whole person, a being whose 'condition' is created by physical, psychological, social and spiritual factors, inextricably woven together. On occasion, Jesus might indeed identify personal sin as the thing which needs 'healing' if the physical cure was to be effective (Matthew 9.2). But at other times healing might also involve being 'cured' of ostracism from the wider community (Zacchaeus, Luke 19.1–9; the Gerasene demoniac, Mark 5.1–20), or the oppression of diabolical forces (the man with an unclean spirit, Mark 1.21–28; the boy with a spirit, 9.14–29). In many cases, of course, healing involves more than one type of 'cure.' Jesus' healing ministry is about something incomparably more profound than the eradication of a set of presenting symptoms. It is about wholeness of life, God's grace making people fully human.[10]

The point is nicely made by the Greek word *sozo*, which often occurs in narratives of Jesus' healings and can refer to the bringing of spiritual 'salvation' or physical 'healing.' In the minds of those writing the gospels, there was no real distinction between the two concepts, for the coming of the kingdom in the person of Jesus Christ necessarily implies both. It is a time of liberation for those captive to all kinds of forces which trap them in a condition of 'sickness.' Thus, a woman, literally bowed down under the oppressive weight of evil is enabled by the touch of Jesus to stand up straight. Bound 'for eighteen long years,' she is at last 'set free from this bondage,' her spiritual release mirrored in physical recovery (Luke 13.10–17).

Healing for All

We have commented that Christians sometimes seem to feel that there is little point in visiting someone with dementia when there is so much else to do. In the light of this, it is a striking feature of the accounts of the synoptic gospels that those whom Jesus heals are almost invariably people deemed unsalvageable by their society—sinners, the chronically sick, foreigners. Scandalously, the gospel writers insist that healing and salvation are intended *especially* for such people. In God's kingdom it is the irredeemable and the irretrievably lost who are brought home as the true heirs of Abraham (Luke 13.16; 14.15–24).

The reason which Jesus commonly gives for choosing to heal such people is their 'faith' (Mark 5.34; 10.52; Luke 7.9; 18.42, etc). But such faith is not arid, bookish belief in 'orthodoxy.' That is the 'faith' only of scribes and Pharisees. Rather, what Jesus detects in those he heals is a desire for restored relationship with the living God, faith understood as trust in Jesus' ability to heal and a readiness to receive that healing. Faith like this is found in unexpected places—not among the articulate religious professionals, but in a sinful woman (Luke 7.50), a Samaritan leper (17.19), or a Roman soldier (7.9).

Jesus, we might say, heals people who *live by* the values of the kingdom of God, rather than articulating them. As people who are marginalized and despised, they live day-to-day in humility and dependence on God. They are people whose identity as human beings is made possible not by the approval of their peers but by the relationship offered to them in Jesus, and his Father's name.

Conclusions

What, then, should we take from this brief survey of Jesus' healings for our own pastoral theology? Perhaps three conclusions might be offered. Firstly, pastoral ministry involves getting close to the unloved. Jesus got close enough to touch, and that touch was both a sign and means by which people were restored to authentic humanity. Jesus Christ is *the* Incarnation of God, but all ministry in his name should be broadly 'incarnational'—a proclamation of Christ in word and deed which is not ashamed to touch the untouchable and embrace the undesirable. Secondly, we need to recognize that 'healing' is not limited to the eradication of physical symptoms. Healing implies wholeness in body, mind, spirit, and relationships. The offer of relationship is itself a form of healing. And finally, we need to accept that Christ offers healing to all kinds of people, including—no, *especially!*—to people that others believe can never receive it.

Let us try to take these conclusions to the chapter which follows.

5
An Inclusive Theological Vision

First Steps in Pastoral Theology

A crucial first step for a pastoral theology must be genuine engagement with the experience of dementia and the *person* who experiences it. As we saw in chapter four, Jesus' ministry was profoundly incarnational. He met needy people as flesh and blood, healing them in all aspects of their being, making them whole. Any theology which analyses, categorizes, and explains human nature solely by reference to its constituent parts (such as the rational faculties or ability to relate to others) is inadequate. There 'is no indication at all that God is a rationalist whose care is a function of indicators of our personhood, or of our achievement within those capacities.'[11] Just as the task of the doctor has been said to be 'to move the world of illness from the unknown to the known world where it can become the subject of human care,' so a task of the Christian theologian might be to describe what it is to be human and put us all in a position to value ourselves and our neighbour.[12]

If we try to write about what being human means but forget we are writing about ourselves and people we love, then we are fooled and demeaned. To know 'humanity' is always to know real people and our real selves. In Christian understanding, true knowledge of humanity (like authentic knowledge of God) comes through love, and is found in relationship, not fact.[13] To attempt to 'know' by comparing and contrasting—by objectifying, quantifying, and perhaps dismissing others—puts such distance between ourselves and them that we are prevented from truly knowing God in other people.

Yet, as we have sensed, this is exactly how theology has often proceeded. To caricature a little, Christians have stood at a distance, pointed at the unfamiliar shapes of people suffering from dementia, and enquired in a careless tone whether it is possible that they are still human. It may have been better to begin by *loving* those people, assuming that humanity persists through the experience of dementia and asking what we can learn from this.

Rediscovering the Image of God

If there is any truth at all in the belief that our identity as humans somehow rests on the identity of God, then we might think that theology has sometimes engaged in presumption on a grand scale. For in presuming to define what is 'God-like' in our fellow human beings, it has implied that God is only to be seen in certain human types and capabilities. Theologically and pastorally, it is crucial we never make the mistake of thinking we have even part of God's nature neatly defined.

16

The true and living God—and so each real, living human—is not to be trapped in this way. He is a God whose essential identity is simply 'I am who I am' (Exodus 3.14–15), an assertion of uniqueness and ultimate mysteriousness.[14] Humanity made in God's image is (as Karl Rahner expressed it) inextricably 'grounded in the abyss of ineffable mystery.'[15] We 'are' as human beings only because we have been spoken into being by God, and restored through Christ. Or, as St Paul expresses it, 'by the grace of God I am what I am' (1 Cor 15.10).

This insistence on God's ultimate mysteriousness should force us to think twice before we allow any statement which denies particular groups or individuals the status of 'authentic humanity.' The persons of the Trinity, Three-in-One, offer a model in which God is to be found in the diversity of community. 'Engaged' theology must begin by being open to the mysterious divine image in all human beings, in 'the incalculable pluralism' of their natures.[16] No one of us can claim that fellow human beings are lesser or 'non-people' because of disability or incapacity. All humanity falls short of the glory of God—that is of its potential eschatological fulness—for all are disabled by sin (Rom 3.9–20). As Christians, we must take seriously the variety of ways in which people are human (including those who do not fit the norm of the independent adult), in the belief that the image of God is only to be found in 'abled' and disabled together.[17] Both university professors and dementia sufferers have something to teach us about living as human beings.

Human Being, Human Weakness

It is in the later stages of illness that many people find it most difficult to see the person behind the dementia. Think of Doris, a stalwart of the local Methodist church for sixty years, constantly in tears because she has 'lost her little boy' and cannot find the bus home, wandering up and down the corridors with her petticoats hanging down round her ankles, trying every door, squatting on the plant pot in a lounge full of people because she cannot find a toilet. What is human about an existence like this?

No one could ever pretend that such an existence is anything other than distressing for Doris and heart-breaking for the rest of us. But is denial of Doris's humanity really the only strategy for coping with such suffering? Surely not. We must say much more than that, and even begin to make the case that Doris with dementia has something to teach us about being human, just as she did before her illness. For example, if it is right to locate humanity essentially in relationship, then we could see Doris as someone who is expressing what it is to live by 'faith alone.' As we saw from Jesus' healings, the theological concept of 'faith,' properly understood, implies not a rational decision between two alternatives but an attitude of wholly open trust towards another. The life of dependency in dementia models faith as relationship, and could be seen as a more perfect way of being human. When Doris seizes your arm as you walk up the corridor and

17

begs you to help her, you see humanity open to and dependent on others, realized without regard to social status, false pride or dignity. It is, perhaps, something of what Jesus meant when he spoke of the need to become like a little child to enter the kingdom (Mark 10.13–16).

This is not an attempt to argue that it is somehow 'good' to suffer from dementia, nor to deny the immense tragedy which its onset produces in individual lives. But neither is it helpful to let our sense of tragedy so overwhelm us that we lose sight of the human existence which can persist even through the experience of dementia. Suffering is part of the human condition—it does not obliterate humanity.

Christ Has Died! Christ Is Risen!

If Christ himself is to be seen as the revelation of humanity in all its fullness, then it is important that we pay proper attention to Christ crucified *and* risen. The scandal of the cross is that what 'is most authentically human…is what is closest to the experiences of birth and death—namely weakness and suffering.'[18] It is as Jesus stands scourged, mocked and bound that Pilate, saying more than he knows, exclaims *'ecce homo!',* 'Behold the man!' (John 19.5). Sickness and wasting are aspects of the human condition, however unpalatable the facts may be.

And yet the humanity imaged in Christ is not destroyed by the sufferings and incapacities of the flesh, for it is humanity which rests on a future hope. The truth of the incarnation, cross and resurrection is that humanity has been offered a new possibility of relationship with God and can hope to transcend its 'natural,' fallen condition in which suffering and limitation play inescapable parts. The mystery of authentic humanity in Christ is the mystery of a being who is *capax et incapax*, possessed of 'capacity in incapacity.'[19] Humanity with Christ is fallen, failing, suffering, limited, but lives in the hope of healing.

It is a task of Christian theology to hold human capacity and incapacity together. For when theology turns away from people whose existence proclaims human dependency, vulnerability and finitude, it turns away from our own humanity. The marginalization of the dementia sufferer is a tragedy for people with dementia, but a further tragedy for all of us as we fail to cope with these witnesses to the reality of our natural state. In the process of turning away, the humanity of both groups is diminished: the dementia sufferer is denied the status of person, and the one who denies it misses the lesson that it is *only* because we are never self-sufficient and self-contained that we are authentically human. Only when we are weak are we truly strong, for it is in weakness that Christ, the authentic image of God, dwells in us (2 Cor 12.9–10).

Human Being in the Sacraments

The capacity in incapacity, or strength in weakness, which underlies our humanity is celebrated by the church in its sacraments of baptism and Communion. Baptism is the sacrament of initiation in which we are accepted in weakness, taken in Christ through the ultimate brokenness of death, and reborn as fully human, in renewed relationship with God. 'Dying to sin that we may live his risen life' (as the Church of England's baptism service expresses it), we find that 'we have a new dignity' and are called by God 'to fullness of life.'

Of course baptism into the death of Christ does not mean that we escape suffering and death. However, our new birth does enable us to participate in new life which is eternal. In baptism, human existence is delivered from the bitterness of the countless 'living deaths' it endures, for it is formed in unbreakable relationship with God. Whatever indignities and incapacities dementia sufferers must face they can never become less than human, for they are now known by God, given 'Christian names' as a sign of their identity as children of God in Christ. At baptism we 'turn to Christ,' and find 'I—Thou' relationship reaching out to draw us in.

If baptism is a sacramental sign which once and for all establishes our humanity, then Communion is a sacrament which repeatedly celebrates it. Here, we are again taken through the movement from death to life in Christ—exodus, Last Supper, crucifixion, resurrection, a banquet for the end of time. In baptism, we were initiated into a salvation-history which became our own story. Participation in Communion reaffirms our participation. Remembering Christ's death on the cross and his resurrection, we receive physical tokens of our inclusion in a covenant-relationship forged in suffering and death, in flesh and in blood.

The 'remembering' which happens at Communion is, however, of a special sort. For although the sacrament is one in which remembering is central, it is not dependent on any one person's capacity to remember. These memorials of the Last Supper are celebrated not by isolated individuals but face-to-face, in 'I—Thou' relationship. The church claims to be a eucharistic community—the 'body of Christ' into which we were baptized. It is not as individuals make intellectual connections between their own stories and the story of Christ that human identity is re-discovered and celebrated. Rather, it is as the community remembers, the body of Christ together, that individuals find their place within the community of redeemed humanity and (like Levi and his fellow pariahs) are 'healed.'

All this means that although the claim to authentic humanity on the part of the dementia sufferer is focused preeminently in the sacraments of baptism and Communion, the reality of that relationship is of little comfort if the church too, as a remembering community, does not recognize and acknowledge it. Where people with severe dementia can no longer remember their own identity, the church must do it for them. 'They may not "know" who they are, but the church knows who they are.'[20] Known by God, they need also to be known by a church which recognizes that they are fully human. Communion only makes sense as a demonstration of the belief that 'we are' in communion with God and each other.

'O love that wilt not let me go'

Perhaps this is the beginnings of an answer to that question of Greg's which first made me think about the church's care of people with dementia. 'What are we doing here,' giving communion to people who cannot even recognize our presence? We are offering tokens of God's superfluous love to people who are weak, vulnerable, and lost. We are reasserting the identity of the person with dementia as someone loved by God, against our tendency to restrict the capacity to be loved, and so to be human, to those who can give a rational response.

Communion is God's gift to us, for God's love is prepared to be wasteful, hopeless and unreturned. As Christians seem to waste their time at the bedside of someone who can no longer communicate or comprehend, they are literally embodying Christ, the starting-point of the Christian understanding of humanity. In the greeting touch of their hand on the dementia sufferer's arm is the healing touch of Christ. All at once, 'I am' not because 'I think' but because I am loved.

6
Pastoral Care for the Person with Dementia

If it does nothing else, I hope this booklet persuades you that gentle neglect of people with dementia is not a worthy pastoral strategy for the church. I hope that you might even have been filled with a new determination to make the needs of dementia sufferers a priority in the church to which you belong. Many readers might feel nervous or inadequately equipped to do this effectively, and so this final chapter is intended to offer some practical suggestions on ministering to people with dementia. Not all the suggestions will apply in every case, of course. Not only are individuals unique, but the course of their condition obviously varies as well and everyone's needs are different.

Visiting

Given everything that has been said in this booklet, it hardly needs to be restated that the most important thing about visiting the person with dementia is just to *do it*! Living with dementia is a very isolating experience. Not only does the illness itself make contact with the world more difficult, but friends, social networks, and even family may move out of reach. People with dementia can be lonely whether they are in a busy nursing home with staff rushed off their feet or at home with a tired and stressed relative. All of us need proper relationships with other people to grow as human beings and tend to regress when we lack quality contact. Spending time with a person suffering from dementia is about more than showing relatives that the church cares; it is a way of affirming and bettering the value of someone's existence.

So try not to be scared or embarrassed about visiting someone with dementia. Your presence is highly unlikely to upset them and will, in most cases, be appreciated. If someone you are visiting becomes distressed, anxious, or aggressive and you cannot reassure them, then just stay calm and friendly and say goodbye. Their agitation is unlikely to be caused by anything terrible you have said or done, so go back again another time.

Of course it is important to check with carers that the time of your visit is convenient. Many people with dementia are more confused early in the morning or later in the evening, and those who look after them may well be able to give advice on what time of day is likely to produce the most worthwhile visit. Whatever time you go, it is a good idea not to let your visit run on for too long—it will be as exhausting for the person you are visiting as it is for you! On the other hand, do not let carers or relatives persuade you that it is not worth visiting. Try and reassure them that you will not be upset or wrong-footed by what you find.

Communicating

Communicating with someone suffering from dementia can be difficult, though often conversation will flow more easily than you would guess. Most dementia sufferers, of course, are likely to be elderly and it is worth remembering basics such as speaking clearly, finding as quiet a place as possible, and making sure hearing aids and teeth are in! Comprehension, speech or both are commonly affected by dementia, so give conversation time. Avoid using complex sentence constructions, and try not to ask several questions in one go. Asking things which require a factual response can be more helpful than asking open questions ('would you like sugar?' rather than 'how do you like your tea?'). Where someone is struggling for a forgotten name or word, do not leap in instantly with your guess, but be prepared to prompt where necessary. Do not forget the immense value of non-verbal communication either. Appropriately used, touch can be worth a thousand half-understood words. Smile. Point to things you are talking about. If you are ordained, wear a dog-collar as a visual clue.

It is always difficult to know when it is right to correct someone who is muddled in their conversation. Sometimes a little gentle reorientation can be appreciated and valuable. For example, someone who has guessed that if you are the vicar then today must be Sunday will probably be grateful if you tell them that in fact it is Wednesday. Such reorientation needs to be done sensitively, however. There is no need to correct every inaccuracy, and doing so can be distressing for the person you are talking to—you will be merely advertising their confusion. A better approach can be to try and read the concern or emotion lying behind the outward form of the words, an approach sometimes called 'validation.' For instance, if a woman you are visiting in hospital repeatedly states 'I must go home—my husband needs his dinner,' you could reply 'he's dead and you're in hospital so cannot go home'—but it *might* be better to try and pick up on her anxiety about someone she loves.

Some conversations with someone who suffers from dementia can feel bizarre, but do not be put off. Your very participation is a good thing. Do not assume someone with dementia is incapable of understanding you, even where they have real problems communicating a response. Try to avoid the habit which so many carers fall into (I speak from personal guilt) of talking over the person with dementia. Your colleague may indeed be more fascinating and comprehensible, but it is highly disrespectful to the person whom you are treating as if he or she did not exist.

Worship[21]

It is a scandal if people with dementia are denied the chance to participate in worship. It is through worship that we renew our experience of God and are united with the rest of his people. Worshipping with people suffering from dementia can be very powerful for us. It can also be comforting for them, and a rare chance to participate in something on equal terms. For all these reasons, it is well worth trying. My suggestions here concentrate on worship designed especially for people with dementia (for example, in a nursing home), but try asking yourself first of all whether it is *really* impossible for someone to worship with everyone else in the local church. The difficulties are frequently exaggerated.

Hosting a good service for people with dementia rests on many of the same principles that were outlined above. Christian worship makes frequent use of visual symbolism, so use visual clues to reinforce a sense that 'church' is happening here—candles, a cross, robes, or whatever is in your tradition. Remember to announce at the start of a service who you are, where everyone is, and what you are all there for.

Because dementia makes it difficult to assimilate new information, it is generally helpful to use familiar liturgies, words, and tunes, though you can still be creative with how you use them. Listening to a woman whose short-term memory was around thirty seconds singing six verses of a hymn word-perfectly taught me how amazingly persistent the memory for things said or done in church over a lifetime can be. Readings and prayers should be fairly short and simple, and generally reassuring in tone. There is no need to omit preaching entirely, but any address should be *very* short. Try and keep the whole service to a maximum of half an hour. If people wander off, before then, that is fine. Just try to ensure you have some help in the room to sort out the inevitable minor disturbances. If the service involves Communion, then consider in advance potential difficulties with chewing or swallowing. A glass of water may be helpful but consider also breaking wafers or bread into smaller pieces, giving by intinction, or giving communion in one kind only.

Further Reading and Help

P Barham and R Hayward, *From the Mental Patient to the Person* (London and New York: Routledge, 1991)

A Jewell (ed), *Spirituality and Ageing* (London: Jessica Kingsley, 1999)

T Kitwood, *Dementia Reconsidered. The Person Comes First* (Buckingham: Open University Press, 1997)

S Pattinson, *Pastoral Care and Liberation Theology* (Paperback edition, London: SPCK, 1997)

S G Post, *The Moral Challenge of Alzheimer's Disease* (2nd edition, Baltimore and London: John Hopkins University Press, 2000)

G D Weaver, 'Senile dementia and a resurrection theology,' *Theology Today* 42 (1986)

The Dementia Services Development Centre produces a wide range of interesting materials, including reading lists and reports. Contact DSDC, University of Stirling, Stirling, FK49 4LA (www.stir.ac.uk/dsdc). Methodist Homes for the Aged together with the Christian Council on Ageing have produced various pamphlets giving advice on visiting and worship for people with dementia. Contact Epworth House, Stuart Street, Derby, DE1 2EQ. Local branches of The Alzheimer's Disease Society and Age Concern should be able to point you towards contacts and resources.

Notes

1   *Ageing: Report of the Social Policy Committee of the Board for Social Responsibility* (London: Church House Publishing, 1990) p 91.
2   *Living in the Labyrinth: A Personal Journey Through the Maze of Alzheimer's* (Mainsail Press: Cambridge, 1994) p 75.
3   T Kitwood, *Dementia Reconsidered: The Person Comes First* (Buckingham: Open University Press, 1997).
4   E L Mascall, *The Importance of Being Human* (London: Oxford University Press, 1959) p 57.
5   E Brunner, *Man in Revolt. A Christian Anthropology* (London and Redhill: Lutterworth Press, 1939) p 480 (my emphasis).
6   E Brunner, *The Christian Doctrine of Creation and Redemption: Dogmatics Vol II* (London: Lutterworth Press, 1952) p 57.
7   M Büber, *I and Thou* (Edinburgh: Clark, 1937). The pages of Barth are notoriously many, but those most influential on my thinking are *Church Dogmatics* III, part i, *The Doctrine of Creation*, G W Bromiley and T F Torrance (eds), (Edinburgh: T & T Clark, 1958) pp 182–6.
8   R S Anderson, *On Being Human: Essays in Theological Anthropology* (Grand Rapids: Eerdmans, 1982) p 39.
9   For a thorough survey of ground not covered here, try E Hill, *Being Human: A Biblical Perspective* (Chapman: London, 1984).
10 *A Time to Heal: A Report for the House of Bishops on the Healing Ministry* (Church House Publishing: London, 2000) p 24.
11 P Ramsey, *Ethics on the Edge of Life* (London: Yale University Press, 1978) p 205.
12 S Hauerwas, *Suffering Presence* (Notre Dame: University of Notre Dame Press, 1986) p 49.
13 J D Zizioulas, 'Human capacity and incapacity: a theological exploration of personhood,' *Scottish Journal of Theology* 28 (1975), 426.
14 J Goldingay, 'Being human,' in F Young (ed), *Encounter with Mystery. Reflections on L' Arche and Living with Disability* (London: DLT, 1997) p 138.
15 K Rahner, *Foundations of Christian Faith* (New York: Crossroad Publishing, 1995) p 42.
16 K Rahner 'Man (anthropology) III. Theological,' in Rahner (ed), *Encyclopedia of Theology: A Concise Sacramentum Mundi* (London: Burns and Oates, 1975) p 892.
17 Goldingay, 'Being human,' pp 133–4.
18 R Sharkey, 'L' Arche: the community and its relationship to society,' in Young (ed), *Encounter with Mystery*, pp 61–2.
19 Zizioulas, 'Human capacity,' 430.
20 S Hauerwas, 'What could it mean for the Church to be Christ's body? A question without a clear answer,' *Scottish Journal of Theology* 48 (1995), 10.
21 In addition to what follows, see M Goodall, 'Worshipping with those who have Dementia,' in A Jewell (ed), *Spirituality and Ageing* (London: Jessica Kingsley, 1999).